Options Trading

Option Trading Strategies For Beginners

Table of Contents

Introduction

Should you invest in stock or options?

This is a common question among most investors. The thing is that options can be more beneficial than stock. But at the same time, they are just as risky. The decision to get involved in trading them depends on your goals as well as your willingness to monitor the market.

When trading options, it is important to weigh each decision so that it leads to the best possible outcome. And that can only happen in regard to how much knowledge you have about options.

In this book, you will learn the basics of options trading. We will start with an introduction to what options are, their types, and benefits. We will then move on to the risks. You will find another chapter that talks about investment strategies – saying you need to understand this part of the book is an understatement.

So without further ado, let's get started.

Chapter 1: Options 101

An option is simply an agreement or contract that gives a buyer a right trade a security at a set price prior to an agreed expiration date.

One key point of this definition is "right that the buyer" has. This means he or she has the freedom to trade the security without being forced by anyone or any rule.

When we talk of an underlying security, we refer to stock, indexes, or other similar products. If stock is used as the security being traded, it means the buyer has a right to trade shares of a certain company whenever he decides. And the shares are bought or sold at a price agreed during the purchase of the option.

Another significant part of the definition is that the option has an expiry date. Once this is reached, the option loses its value. In other words, it cannot be used to buy or sell stock.

Trade always involves two parties and options trading is no exception. In this case, the other party is the seller or writer. Unlike the buyer who has a right, the seller has an obligation to trade the security if the buyer decides to use the option. The seller is the one who assumes the greatest risk. And as such, the buyer must pay him a premium–the sum of money that buys the option. The seller keeps this amount whether the option is exercised or not.

Features of an Option Contract

Every option has these features:

Underlying security: mostly, this refers to shares. But there are other times where it may represent other forms of equity.

Contract size: assuming the underlying security are shares, one option usually represents 100 shares.

Strike price: The price at which an security must be traded between the buyer or seller.

Expiry date: The buyer must, if he chooses, use them before the expiry date.

Premium: this amount is reached through negotiation between the buyer and the writer.

Types of Options

There are 2 types of options. What you buy depends on what you want to achieve with the option:

Call Option

This allows the buyer to trade a security that has a strike price on prior to the expiry date.

For example, imagine a company currently trading at $2 per share. You can buy a call option for $25 ($0.25 per share) that has a strike price of $3. Since you are buying, you will have to give $25 to the seller as premium. If the price per share rises to $5, you can use your option. The seller will have to sell you 100 shares at $3. If he currently does not have them, he will have to buy them at $5 each and sell them to you.

Put Option

A put option lets the you trade a security at a strike price before the expiry date.

For instance, if you own shares you believe will drop in price, you can buy a put option. Again, you will pay the seller a premium, which he will keep either you use the option or not. We can assume your shares currently trade at $5 per share, and that the strike price is $4. If the market price drops to $2 per share, you can use your option. The seller will be obliged to buy your shares at $4 each.

Option Styles

Options can be exercised in two styles: American or European. The American style says that you can use your option at any time as long as it's before the expiry date. The European style, on the other hand, allows you to only exercise your option on the day of expiration.

Many prefer the American style because of its flexibility.

Benefits of Options

Options are great tools for investors. They offer benefits you may miss if you buy the actual stock or any other asset they represent:

Hedging – if you have stock with a market price suspected to fall, you can buy put options to decrease your losses. In fact, if the strike price is more than

13

the amount you purchased the stock for, your loss will be limited to the premium you have to pay the seller.

Make huge profits –They provide high returns on investments than if you buy the actual stock.

	Option	Stock
Bought: January 2000	50	660
Sold: March 2000	82	715
Profit	32	55
Return on Investment	64%	8.33%

You do not require a lot of capital – options cost a fraction of the investment you would have made if you bought the actual stock.

Profit during booms or declines – movement in stock price, whether up or down, can increase the value of your

14

option depending on its type. This is
unlike stock which is only attractive
when its price goes up.

Chapter 2: Basic Terminology

Most of the words used in options are similar to those used when trading stocks. However, there are others that only apply to options. And you must ensure that you know these really well as it's the best way to accelerate your learning progress. At the same time, it's also a guarantee that you won't miss important facts when you start trading.

In this chapter, we will focus on some of the words you are likely to meet when you start trading options.

Long – this word shows ownership of a certain security or option. When you purchase stock or an option, you are considered to be "long."

Short – this is the opposite of "long." And in that regard, it indicates that you do not have ownership of a particular option. When you write an option – you are considered to be "short."

In-the-Money – This refers to when a stocks price is above the strike price.

Think of it in this way: when your option is in-the-money, the conditions for exercising it are in your favor.

Out-of-the-Money – Put options are out-of-the-money when the price of a stock increases over the strike price.

Think of it in this way: holding an option that's out-of-the-money means conditions don't favor you to exercise.

At-the-money – this refers to all options, calls or puts, with the strike price equal to the stock price.

Time value – this is the perceived value of the time left on an option before it will expire

Taker or holder – another name for the buyer of the option.

Exercise – refers to when the buyer uses the right stipulated in the contract.

Assignment – when the buyer exercises, the seller is said to have been assigned.

Open – one is said to have opened a position when he writes or buys an option.

Close – this is when you trade an option to cancel a position you opened earlier.

Chapter 3: Risks of Options Trading

Options are not for everyone. As such, you must assess your objectives as well as financial position before you buy or write one. Experience is one important characteristic you need if you are to be successful. But since you are just getting started, you can make up for that by absorbing everything you can concerning options. While this won't eliminate the risk, you will know what to do to manage it.

In this chapter, we will look at the dangers associated with options.

Risk of losing your whole investment –buying options requires that you pay a premium. And the higher this amount, the higher the risk associated with your investment. The problem is that markets always change. And in some cases, they may go in opposition to what you predicted. As a result, your option may represent a loss, eliminating any chances that you may exercise it. Making things worse, time is always running against you. If you let your option expire, the writer will be the winner as he will keep the premium.

Loss in time value – as options get closer to their expiration, they lose their time value. So you must keep on assessing them to ensure that there is still sufficient time to realize your goals.

Risk of restrictions on your options – although you have rights to exercise your options, some agencies can impose restrictions at any time. These would make it impossible to profit from opportunities that may arise in the market.

Big risk for writers – writing an option automatically presents a big risk to your finances. Even though you receive a premium, the loss you may incur if assigned may be bigger. Remember, as a writer, you are obliged to meet your end of the contract if the buyer chooses to exercise his right. What makes this even scarier is that the buyer will keep his eyes open for the most profitable opportunities. Usually, these will be the worst moments you will pray against as a writer.

Need to provide funds to your broker in advance – if you write an option, you may be assigned at any time. To ensure that you meet your obligation, your broker may request funds in advance to use in buying or selling the underlying security. Because of this, you will have less capital to invest in other ventures until you close your position. But on the flip side, this is an advantage; there is no chance of getting into other deals that may leave you with no money.

Requires dedication and time – one of the biggest requirements about options trading, if you want to be successful, is to fully understand the

21

strategies. Although some of these are simple, the best ones are complicated. You will need to dedicate a lot of time to master them. You must be ready to spend hours of reading, analyzing, and applying what you learn in practice models. Consequently, this will reduce the time you spend on other things. And when you finally start trading, you will need to raise your dedication even higher.

Chapter 4: Fundamental and Technical Analysis

Option contracts have expiry dates, which is one of their biggest disadvantages. So before you buy or sell one, you must ensure that it will achieve your goal and in the stated time frame. Without this, you may make losses. In the worst cases, you may lose your whole investment.

Prior to trading an option, you must have a good sense of what might happen to the market in future. Although you can use intuition to determine this, it helps to use proven techniques that others have been following for years. These techniques are two: fundamental and technical analysis.

Fundamental Analysis

This is what most new investors learn. The method determines a company's investment worthiness by looking at its performance. However, this decision rests on your belief that the company will continue to grow.

Here are examples of things you need to focus on:

Results: this looks at how the company has been performing in the past. As already said, you look at growth in profits, a strong market share, good competitive advantage, and other things.

Management: you need to prove that the management of the company is capable of delivering profitable results. And most importantly, you must believe that it will take the company to new heights.

Industry: dying industries are not ideal for investment. It's why most investors fight to invest in industries that are growing. Like at the moment, emerging industries worth looking at include male grooming, virtual reality, wind energy, and food e-commerce.

Economy: in a falling economy, companies struggle. As a result, share prices drop. It is, therefore, not surprising that people invest in put options in such economies. For instance, if unemployment rises, a lot of people have no money as they don't have jobs. Those who work save every dollar in fear of what may happen if they get laid-off. Because of this, consumer spending, especially on non-essential goods like leisure, falls. Companies in the affected industries face declining share prices.

News: what's reported on the news, as well as recommendations from analysts, play a big role in people's investment decisions. That is why news is one area that fundamental analysis is concerned with. However, know that it is a mistake to base your decisions on the recommendations of analysts; you will be misled.

The point of fundamental analysis is not to predict what the future will be like. Rather, it is to enable you to recognize the market direction based on the available data.

Technical Analysis

This lies in opposition to fundamental analysis. Technical analysis is all about identifying trends in the price of securities by looking at charts. That's the reason many call it "chart reading." However, that should not fool you to underestimate it or think it is simple. From the charts, further ratios are developed which aid in analyses.

A trend in the market price of a security can either be upward or downward. Technicians believe that by analyzing the trend, you automatically consider all the other factors that affect the company; so you have no need to look in what industry the company is in, let alone what it does.

Technicians agree that price movements do not just happen randomly. So if you recognize a pattern where the stock price of a certain company drops then rises, you can buy shares during dips hoping to profit from the rise later on.

Although these two approaches are different, most experts agree that you can get better results by combining them. But before you do that, you need to dedicate time to really understand how each of them works.

Another issue that comes up is figuring out which companies you must start with in your analyses. One way to do this is to listen to the news. You need to know which industries are booming, which companies are struggling, etc.

Chapter 5: Basic Investing Strategies

Investing in options is a risky way of making money; therefore, you must be clear of your goals with each move you make. It is crucial that you choose the best strategy depending on your situation. Whether you are expanding your portfolio or protecting it from market decline, you must carefully assess the implications of your decisions. Do not just buy or write options out of impulse – you will make mistakes.

The broader your knowledge on this subject, the greater the freedom when investing.

Call Buying

This is one of the simplest strategies to implement. And it's also among the easiest to understand. Using an investor's terminology, you have a bullish outlook (believing that market price for the shares will rise.)

You have either of these objectives when buying a call:

1. To lower the price of a share

Here is an example:

You can purchase a call option that has a strike price of $50 that costs of $300. If you were to buy these shares now, assuming they are trading at $48 per share, you would have to pay $4800 for 100 shares. But because of the option, you will pay $300 for a guarantee to buy them anytime at $50 per share.

Imagine a situation where the share price rises to $55 in 3 months. If buying on the market, you would have to pay $5500. However, because you have a call option, you will pay $5000 since the strike price is $50. Your total investment will be $5300 ($5000 for the shares and $300 for the option). So you will save $200.

2. *Make profits by selling your option* – most call options are sold and not exercised. This is because when an option's intrinsic value rises, its premium also rises.

Let's go back to the above example where you have a call option you bought for $300 with a strike of $50. If the price of the shares increases to $59, you can sell your option for $600, making a profit of $300 (100% return on investment).

You should follow this strategy when you anticipate a boom in the economy. Also, you must target stock of companies that are expected to grow. This is where fundamental and technical analysis becomes handy. However, you must not forget to assess the option's time frame in regard to when the share price will rise. That will determine the likelihood of making a profit.

The best part of this strategy is that your loss is limited to the amount you pay as premium.

Put Buying

This strategy is suitable when you have a bearish outlook (you expect the share price of your stock to fall). By buying a put option, you limit your losses in case share prices fall. And in some situations, you can make a profit despite the fall.

Here are examples:

Suppose you own shares of ABC limited you bought 2 years ago at $48 per share. At the moment, they are trading at $60. From your analyses, you expect this price to drop. And in response, you purchase a put option for $200 that has a strike price of $50.

If ABC shares fall to $45 per share, you are free to exercise your option. Since the strike price is $50, you will receive $5000 for selling your shares. However, from this amount, you must subtract $200 – the premium you paid to buy the option. This will bring the total to $4800 (the same amount you invested 2 years ago in acquiring the shares). If it was not for the option, you would have sold your shares for $4500.

In a different scenario, you may want to keep your shares, believing their prices will increase. In this case, you can sell the option and make a profit from it. The thing is that as share prices drop, a put option's value increases as long as it is in-the-money.

So if the ABC shares continue to drop, anyone will be willing to buy your put option for more than $200.

Puts can either be married or protective. The former refers to put options you buy at the same time you buy stock. The latter means put options you buy for shares you already own.

Call Writing

Being a writer of an option obliges you to fulfill your part of the contract if assigned. And this may be a disadvantage as the market conditions may not be on your side. With this in mind, you may wonder why write call options if they are risky.

Only a senseless buyer would exercise that option as it would be cheaper to buy the shares on the market. So the option will likely expire worthless. And you, as the writer, will profit from the premium.

As you can see, this will earn you some extra cash on top of all the benefits you already get from your shares. Mostly, people who follow this strategy believe that in the short term, the price of their shares will drop and pick up in the future.

But the strategy can backfire if the stock price rises: the possibility of being assigned is very high. In response to this, many close their positions by buying another option in the same series as the one they sold. Unfortunately, this is done at a higher price than the premium they got for selling the option.

In case your option is exercised, you are obliged to provide your shares to your brokerage. However, know that being assigned to a call option does not always result in a loss for you.

Here is an example:

Suppose you bought shares of a BBN limited at $50 a year ago and they are now trading at $60. You can order a call option that is at a SP of $65 and trade at $300. If the share price rises to $70, that option will likely be exercised. And you will make a profit.

Your initial investment a year ago was $5000. Since the option has been exercised, you will receive $6500 ($65 is the strike price). To this, you will need to add the $300 premium you received earlier, bringing the total income to $6800. You will see that you have made a profit of $1800 ($6800 - $5000). However, commissions and other fees are yet to be subtracted from that profit.

In this case, the only disadvantage is that by being assigned, you lose all chances of earning further from the rise in share price.

Call options can either be covered or naked. Covered calls are those options you write on stock you already own. These are better as they are less risky. On the other hand, naked calls are options you write on stock that you do not currently own. And as such, they are very risky, with the possibility of losing much of your investment.

Put Writing

Writing puts is another risky strategy as you may be assigned to buy shares at a higher price than they currently are.

Mostly, when people write put options, they have a bullish behavior. And as such, the buyer will not exercise the option, letting it expire worthless and leaving them with the premium as profit.

Here is an example:

If you believe that stock will not fall below $60, you can write a put option that has a SP at $55 and trade it for $250. Assuming the shares are currently trading at $63, you can bet the option will not be exercised as it is out-of-the-money. In fact, even if the price per share drops to $57, you can still be confident that you will not be assigned.

But the story will change if the price drops below the strike price; you are likely going to be assigned. And depending on the difference between the strike and share price, you may be forced to buy the shares at a loss. As such, this strategy is best for experienced investors.

Another reason you may write a put option is when you want to lock a price at which you would like to buy the shares of a certain company. However, you must carefully analyze your decision to not make a loss in the process.

If you would like to close your position, you can buy the same put. But as expected, this will be at a higher price than what you got as the premium.

Spread Strategy

The 4 strategies we just looked at are the most basic. Since markets do not always turn out as predicted, you may want to reduce your risk by adopting complex strategies – the spread strategy is one example you can think of. With this, you use at least 2 options on the same stock. You may, for example, purchase an option and write another one on the same stock. This would limit your losses if the unwanted happens. And it would also reduce your profit.

A spread strategy requires 2 transactions to be executed at the same time. As a result, the options involved will likely have the same expiry date, the only difference between them being their strike prices. This difference in price is what's known as "the spread."

However, there are cases where the strike prices are similar and the dates are different.

Since stock prices usually fluctuate, you have choices on the type of spread you can use. If you expect a rise in price, you can go for a bull spread.

Applying the spread strategy is not easy, you need to be an experienced investor as there is a lot involved: determining the market direction, monitoring your open positions, calculating your income in each scenario, and more. All this requires extensive knowledge as well as dedication.

Mistakes to Avoid

Although mistakes are great as learning tools, we have to acknowledge that they can also hurt your progress. Another reason you must avoid them is because you have money on the line. Here are some of the common mistakes investors make:

1. Not thinking of being assigned early

Most new investors believe that the buyer will take his time in exercising the option. So they are caught off guard when the opposite happens.

To avoid this, ensure that you have a plan on how you will act if assigned early.

2. Not knowing your exit

Before you open a position, you must know the amount of profit you want to make and the loss you are willing to take. Once you reach those limits, move on to another trade. Being greedy to make more can yield unwanted consequences. And when making losses, hanging around thinking the market will bounce up again may be a waste of time. Do not let emotions get in your way. Do what you planned to do.

3. Buying out of the money options

Investing low and selling high is what most people new to investing thinks makes money. And as a result, they focus on out-of-the-money options. But you must know that these options are cheap for a reason – it's not easy to make money with them.

Chapter 6: Choosing a Broker

You do not need to meet the seller or buyer of an option, your broker handles all that. As such, it is important to choose the right broker. Besides, you are about to trust him with your money – make mistakes during this process and the loss will be yours.

A broker not only executes your orders, but he may also offer advice on the best options to invest in, recommend a strategy, monitor your open positions, and may even manage a portfolio on your behalf.

With the rise of the internet, options are now mostly traded online. And you can bypass the traditional brokers for an online one. The biggest difference between the two is the scope of services you get.

With a traditional broker, the services are wide-ranging, with much focus on advice on how to best invest your money. With most online brokers, you are in charge of everything. You are given all the information you may need to make investment decisions. And it is up to you to decide how to use that info.

As expected, traditional brokers cost more for their customized services. On the other hand, online brokers are usually cheaper.

So before you start looking for a broker, decide which of the two you will go with. If you are inexperienced and have no time to learn everything about options trading, then a traditional broker is the best way to go.

Here are some things you must keep in mind when looking for a broker:

Services offered – don't assume all brokers offer the same services even if they are in the same category. So before you register for an account, really look at all the services you will get. And as a warning, don't go for an impressive list. You will waste money as you may not use some of those services. This is the reason it helps to identify exactly what you want in a broker before you start looking for one.

Fees – brokers charge differently. So compare all fees before you make a decision. Furthermore, you must not forget to dig out hidden fees; for example, account inactivity and annual maintenance fees. And most importantly, remember that cheap usually means a low-quality service – keep this in front of your mind before you go for anything cheap.

Reputation – for your own good, avoid new brokers. You must go for those with a successful record of caring for their clients.

Availability – this mainly applies to online brokers. Remember the adage that "time is money." And when trading options, this is very true. You must ensure that the broker's website is online all the time. In addition to that, it must be able to carry your orders promptly.

Alternate forms of trading – in case the website is down, or you are away from your computer, the broker must have another form of conducting trade. Usually, this may be through telephone.

Good customer support – this is the 21st century and gone are the days when we had to wait for hours to get a response for a problem. The broker you choose must have good customer support. Reading the broker's reviews online is a good way to determine this.

Trust your intuition – that thought in your head telling you to pass a certain broker may have a valid reason for existence. So listen to it. For example, some brokers talk about quick riches to persuade people to open accounts with them. But anyone who knows options trading should be cautious of such claims. Although you can make thousand in months, the process is not as easy as discovering the most profitable companies at the moment.

Chapter 7: Taxation

Taxation can determine whether a certain strategy will work for or against you; therefore, you must take it into consideration before you make any decisions.

Options are taxed in the same way as stocks. However, there are a few things that differ between these two. And it is important that you understand these differences really well.

Holding Period

The length of time you hold your options determines the rate at which they are taxed.

All options you hold for less than 12 months fall in the short-time category. And these are taxed at the same rate as your other incomes (know that most of the options are short term).

Long-term options, on the other hand, are those you hold for more than 12 months. The biggest advantage with these is that they have a lower tax rate than short-term options.

Capital Gains and Losses

These are terms you will come across often when dealing with taxation. Capital gain refers to how much money you earned when you sell your security. However, to that amount, you must not forget to add or subtract premium, transaction costs, and any other fees. This may increase or reduce your capital gain.

The importance of correctly calculating this amount is that it is taxable. The only exceptions are when it is held in a tax-deferred account or when it offsets capital losses.

The tax rate of your capital gain depends on whether it falls into short-term or long-term.

Capital loss means you lost money on your security and as such, it is not taxable. It is added to the capital gain, an act which reduces the amount of tax you have to pay. And in some cases, it may cancel your whole capital gain.

There are a whole bunch of other terms you must be familiar with regarding taxation. Understanding these is crucial as it will reduce the likelihood of tax surprises.

One way to keep up with this subject is to work with a tax advisor. Although this will increase your expenses, the benefit you will get is well worth the money. Actually, most experienced investors work with tax advisors. Not only are these people helpful in simplifying what you may consider complicated terms, but they are also useful for recommending strategies.

You must know that your tax treatment depends on your situation, and an advisor can help clarify this.

That aside, you must keep all records of transactions, positions you close and open, capital gains as well as losses, and anything else you think may be handy during taxation. In addition to this, statements from your brokerage, receipts, as well as email confirmations must be kept. This laborious process can save you headaches and effort during taxation. If you want more advice on what tax info you must keep, ask your tax advisor.

Lastly, you must know which tax form to file and how to file it. If you are in doubt about something, be sure to search for solutions. And if you don't find what you want, don't be shy to ask.

Conclusion

First things first, thank you for getting to the end of the book. We hope you found it helpful. Having come this far, we urge you to remember and use your new found knowledge. However, the journey does not end here. The learning must continue: read articles on the web, attend trading events, listen to the news, etc.

In addition, you must seek advice from experienced traders on things you do not understand.

One thing to never forget is that you must not make decisions based on emotions. Everything must be carefully screened, with its implications as well as advantages understood.

To broaden your understanding of options, there are virtual simulators online you can try. Most of these use real market conditions – the only thing different is that you use fake money. So you can test different strategies without sacrificing anything. If you make a mistake, you can happily make amends and see what went wrong.

We wish you good luck in your quest to making money with options.

www.ingramcontent.com/pod-product-compliance
Lightning Source LLC
Chambersburg PA
CBHW070406190526
45169CB00003B/1137